W9-CPF-347

THIS CANDLEWICK BOOK BELONGS TO:

_____

_____

_____

_____

For Rachael and Matthew
J. L.

For Edie and Max
D. D.

Text copyright © 1994 by Dayle Ann Dodds
Illustrations copyright © 1994 by Julie Lacome

First paperback edition 1996

The Library of Congress has cataloged the hardcover edition as follows:

Dodds, Dayle Ann.
The shape of things / Dayle Ann Dodds ;
illustrated by Julie Lacome. — 1st U.S. ed.
ISBN 978-1-56402-224-0 (hardcover)
1. Geometry — Juvenile literature. [1. Shape.]
I. Lacome, Julie, ill. II. Title
QA445.D63   1994
516'.15 — dc20   93-47255
ISBN 978-1-56402-698-9 (paperback)

APS 19 18
35 34

Printed in Humen, Dongguan, China

This book was typeset in Columbus.
The illustrations were done in paper collage.

Candlewick Press
99 Dover Street
Somerville, Massachusetts 02144

visit us at www.candlewick.com

THE SHAPE OF THINGS

Dayle Ann Dodds

illustrated by
Julie Lacome

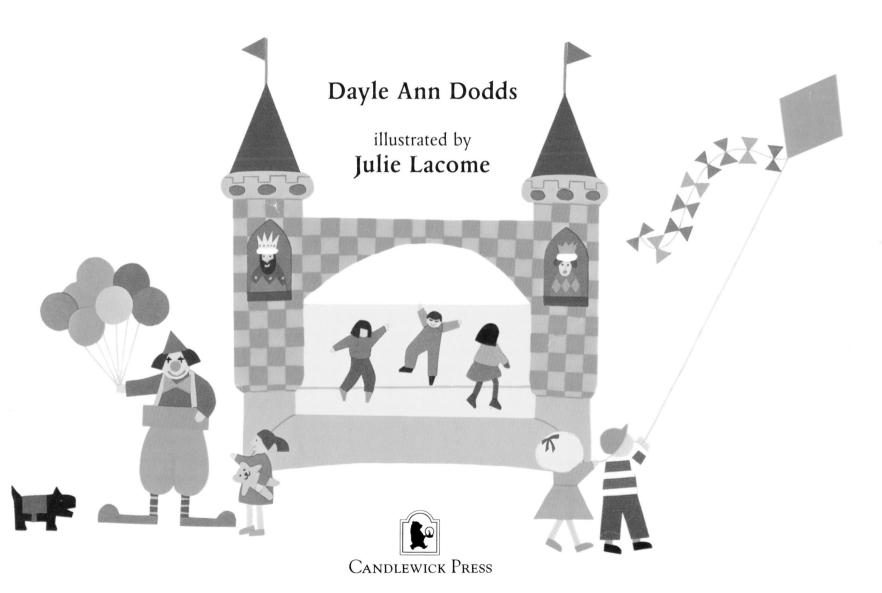

CANDLEWICK PRESS

A square is just a square,
Until you add a roof,
Two windows and a door,
Then it's much, much more!

A circle's just a circle,
Until you add some lights,
Chairs high and low,
Round and round they go.

A triangle's just a triangle,
Until you add another,
An ocean and a sky,
A seagull passing by.

A rectangle's just a rectangle,
Until you add some more,
An engine and a track,
A red caboose in back.

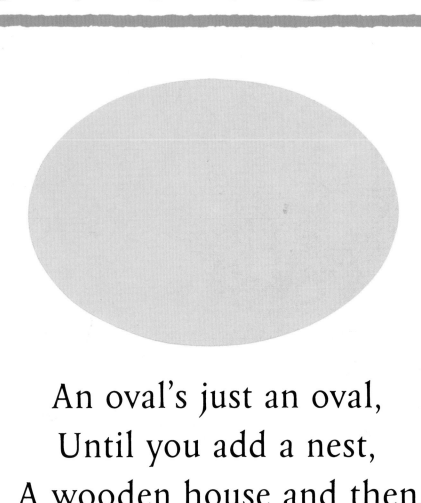

An oval's just an oval,
Until you add a nest,
A wooden house and then
A patient mother hen.

A diamond's just a diamond,
Until you add some string,
Wind and a tail,
Some friends to help it sail.

A shape is just a shape,
But look again and see,

There are shapes of every kind.

How many can you find?

DAYLE ANN DODDS was helping out in a kindergarten class when she developed the idea for *The Shape of Things*. "One child couldn't even begin to draw a picture until I showed him that just two triangles can make a boat. It was amazing how he took it from there and was able to make a very elaborate picture. The idea is really how a few simple shapes make up a lot of things we have in the world." Dayle Ann Dodds is the author of several other children's books.

JULIE LACOME found illustrating *The Shape of Things* to be enjoyable. "For the borders of each page," she says, "I used potato-cut printing, as children do in school — that was the most fun!" Julie Lacome is also the author-illustrator of *Ruthie's Big Old Coat* and the Brand New Readers *Beep, Beep! It's Beeper!* and *Beeper's Friends*.